Sand

Alan Trussell-Cullen

AF605725

Australia • Brazil • Japan • Korea • Mexico • Singapore • Spain • United Kingdom • United States

Sand

Text: Alan Trussell-Cullen
Editor: Ben Haskin
Design: Jennifer Warwick
Series design: James Lowe
Photo researcher: Lisa Piemonte
Production controller: Lisa Porter
Reprint: Siew Han Ong

Acknowledgements
The author and publisher would like to acknowledge permission to reproduce material from the following sources:
Ami-Louise Sharpe: pp. 3, cover; 15 (main);
Getty Images: p. 14 (both); iStockphoto/Craig Cozart: p. 13; iStockphoto/David H Lewis: p. 8; iStockphoto/Owen Price: p. 12; iStockphoto/Robert Bremec: back cover; iStockphoto/Sean Randall: p. 5 (top); Jupiterimages Corporation © 2008: p. 11 (bottom); Newspix/Lisa Clarke: p. 9; Photolibrary: pp. 4 (both), 5 (middle, bottom), 6, 7, 10 (both), 11 (top), 15 (inset).

Every effort has been made to trace and acknowledge copyright. However, if any infringement has occurred, the publishers tender their apologies and invite the copyright holders to contact them.

Fast Forward Independent Texts
Level 11

Text © 2009 Cengage Learning Australia Pty Limited

Copyright Notice
This Work is copyright. No part of this Work may be reproduced, stored in a retrieval system, or transmitted in any form or by any means without prior written permission of the Publisher. Except as permitted under the Copyright Act 1968, for example any fair dealing for the purposes of private study, research, criticism or review, subject to certain limitations. These limitations include: Restricting the copying to a maximum of one chapter or 10% of this book, whichever is greater; Providing an appropriate notice and warning with the copies of the Work disseminated; Taking all reasonable steps to limit access to these copies to people authorised to receive these copies; Ensuring you hold the appropriate Licences issued by the Copyright Agency Limited ("CAL"), supply a remuneration notice to CAL and pay any required fees.

For product information and technology assistance,
in Australia call 1300 790 853;
in New Zealand call 0508 635 766

For permission to use material from this text or product,
please email **aust.permissions@cengage.com**

ISBN 978 0 17 017925 6
ISBN 978 0 17 017896 9 (set)

Cengage Learning Australia
Level 7, 80 Dorcas Street
South Melbourne, Victoria Australia 3205

Cengage Learning New Zealand
Unit 4B Rosedale Office Park
331 Rosedale Road, Albany, North Shore NZ 0632

For learning solutions, visit **cengage.com.au**

Printed in Australia by Ligare Pty Ltd
2 3 4 5 22 21 20

Alan Trussell-Cullen

Contents

CHAPTER 1

What Is Sand?

Sand is made up of millions of very small bits of rock.

Sand that comes from different kinds of rock looks different.

In nature, sand can have many different colours. It can be white, brown, black, yellow, green and even red.

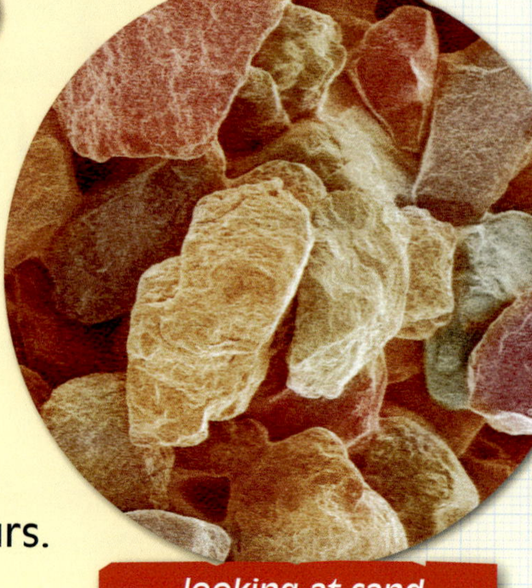

looking at sand through a microscope

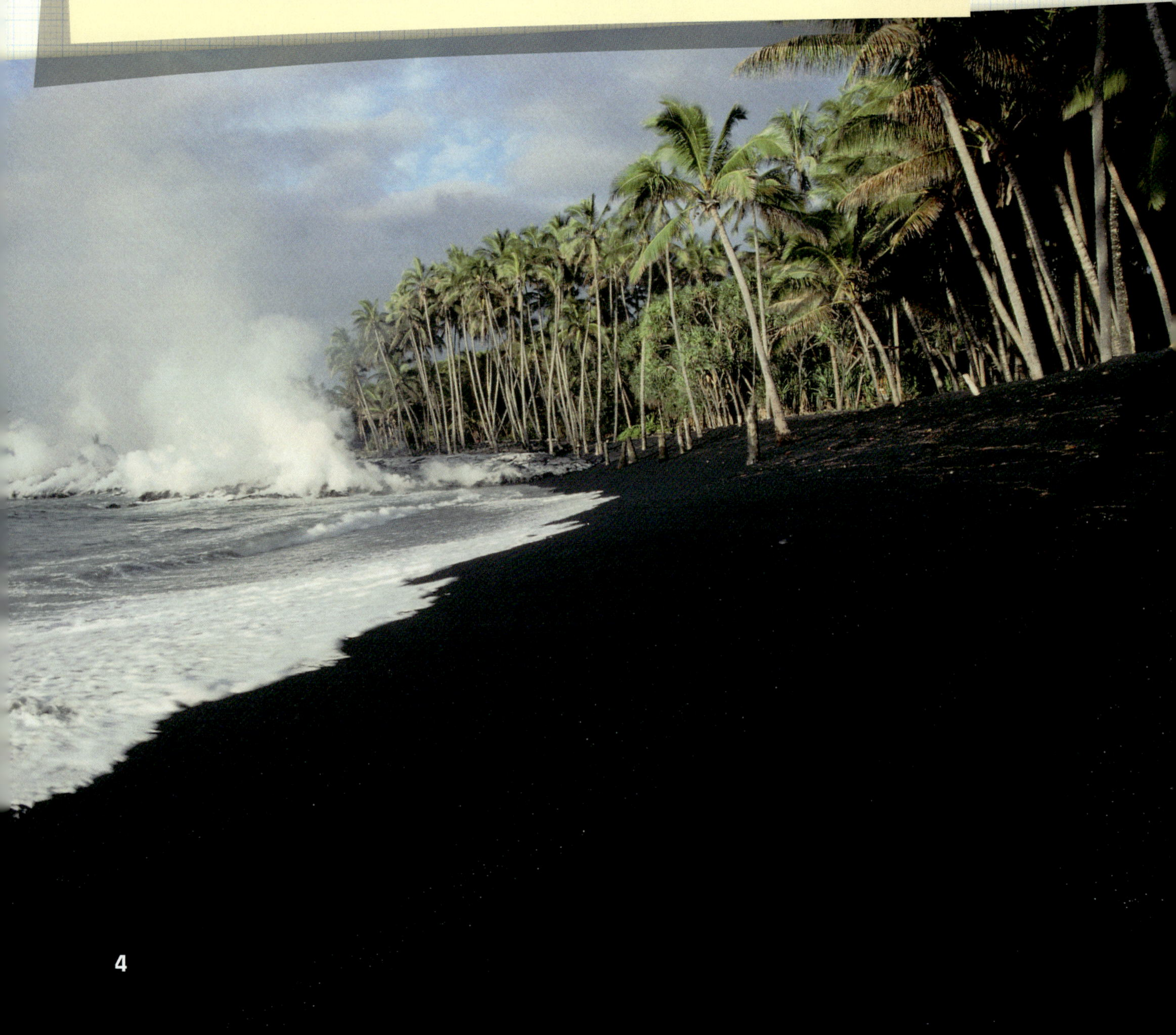

You can find sand in many places.

a sandy desert

sand by a river

a sandy beach

CHAPTER 2

How Is Sand Made?

Over time,
a lot of things help turn rocks into sand.

Sand forms in very windy places.
The wind very slowly wears away rock,
turning it into sand.

These rock shapes formed because wind wore away the rock, creating sand.

Rocks turn into sand in places where it's very cold.

The heat of the sun can also turn rocks into sand.

Waves wear away rock,
turning it into sand.
That's why there's so much sand
at the beach.

CHAPTER 3

Uses for Sand

Sand is used for making a lot of things, like paths, roads and houses.

Sand is used to make concrete.

When there is too much rain,
bags of sand are used to keep water out
of shops and houses.

Sand is also used to make glass. When sand is mixed with other **materials** and heated, it **melts** to make glass.

Glassmakers make some things by blowing air into hot glass.

molten glass

glassblowing

Many of the things we use every day are made of glass. Glass bottles are good for carrying things in.

Windows are made of glass. They keep the wind out, but let in light. They can be made of coloured glass.

Sand is used to make a special kind of paper, called sandpaper.

People use sandpaper
to make things **smooth**.

Sand is also used in machines that take paint off metal or shape hard things, like rock or glass.

using a sand blasting machine

CHAPTER 4

Sand Art and Play

Lots of people like to play with sand. It can be fun to put sand on your friends.

It's also fun to make **art** with sand. People can use different-coloured sand to make sand art.

There are many different kinds of sand art.

Sand sculptures look great, but they don't last long.

Glossary

art	beautiful things
glassmakers	people who make things out of glass
materials	things that are used to make something else
melts	changes from a solid to a liquid
smooth	not rough or bumpy

Index